© 2022 Sovereign Island Publishing

Published by Sovereign Island UK

Sales and Enquires: sovereignislanduk@gmail.com

Contents

WHO IS THE QUEEN?	5
FAMILY	11
HOBBIES AND INTERESTS	23
PALACES AND CASTLES	29
REIGN	32

Who is The Queen?

A queen is a female ruler of an independent state, especially one who inherits the position by right of birth.

1. Queen Elizabeth I was born on 7 September 1533.

2. Queen Elizabeth I was sometimes referred to as the Virgin Queen.

Portrait of Queen Elizabeth I

3. Elizabeth became Queen on 17 November 1558 until her death in 1603.

4. Queen Elizabeth I was the Queen of England and Ireland.

6

5. Elizabeth was the last of the five monarchs of the House of Tudor.

Picture of Red Rose of Tudor

6. Elizabeth's reign became known as the Elizabethan era.

8. Queen Elizabeth was born at Greenwich Palace.

9. Elizabeth caught smallpox in the early 1560s.

10. Queen Elizabeth I was aged 69 at the time of her death, which made her the oldest monarch in British at the time.

11. Queen Elizabeth died in 1603, the same year that the Treaty of Union came into affect.

12. Queen Elizabeth was the last monarch to rule over England before its union with Scotland.

Portrait of King James I

13. James I was Elizabeth I's successor.

Family is a group of persons united by the ties of marriage, blood, or adoption

14. Queen Elizabeth I was named after her grandmothers, Elizabeth of York and Lady Elizabeth Howard.

Picture of King Henry VIII and Anne Boleyn

15. Elizabeth was the daughter of Henry VIII and Anne Boleyn

11

14. Queen Elizabeth I was the second legitimate child of Henry VIII of England

Picture of King Henry VIII statue

15. Elizabeth was the first child of Ann Boleyn.

16. Elizabeth was the heir presumptive to the English throne at birth.

Picture of Queen Elizabeth I praying

17. Elizabeth was baptised on 10th September 1533.

18. Elizabeth's mother Anne Boleyn was beheaded.

Portrait of Anne Boleyn

19. Elizabeth was two years old when her mother was beheaded on 19 May 1536.

14

20. Elizabeth was declared illegitimate after her mother's death and removed from the line of succession.

Portrait of Edward VI

21. Elizabeth had two legitimate half-siblings; Mary and Edward.

22. Elizabeth had many stepmothers.

Portrait of King Henry VIII

23. Elizabeth's father, Henry VIII had six wives.

16

24. Henry VIII's last wife, Catherine Parr, encouraged King Henry to reconcile with Elizabeth and Elizabeth was reinstated into the line of succession.

Portrait of Catherine Parr

25. Catherine Parr also ensured that Elizabeth had a good education.

26. Elizabeth's half brother Edward and half-sister Mary became Edward VI and Mary I.

Picture of Queen Elizabeth I

27. Queen Elizabeth I was the third of Henry VIII children to inherit the throne

28. Elizabeth I never married.

Picture of statue of Elizabeth I

29. Elizabeth I had no children.

19

Family

30. Queen Elizabeth I was the cousin of Mary Queen of Scots.

Portrait of Mary Queen of Scots

31. Elizabeth ordered the execution of Mary, Queen of Scots in 1587.

20

Family

31. Elizabeth was imprisoned in the Tower of London during her sister Mary I's reign as it was believed that she was involved in Wyatt's rebellion.

Picture of the Tower of London

32. Many people believe Elizabeth's mother, Anne Boleyn, was innocent of all charges and her execution was a conspiracy.

21

33. Throughout Elizabeth I's life she wore a locket ring with a hidden picture of her mother inside.

Portrait of Anne Boleyn

34. Elizabeth's stepmother Catherine Parr married her uncle, Thomas Seymour, however Thomas Seymour eventually made advances to Elizabeth.

A hobby is an activity done regularly in one's leisure time for pleasure.

35. Queen Elizabeth I loved horse riding.

36. Queen Elizabeth I is said to have spent hours riding through palace grounds.

23

37. Elizabeth was a firm believer in astrology.

38. Elizabeth kept a personal advisor named John Dee, a renowned mathematician, astronomer, astrologer, and professed alchemist—in her regular company.

24

39. Queen Elizabeth I was passionate about giving food to the poor.

40. As Queen, Elizabeth oversaw the nation's first attempts at poverty relief such as her implementation of 1601 Elizabethan Poor Law.

41. Elizabeth was multi-lingual.

42. Queen Elizabeth I was known to be fluent in French, Italian, and Latin.

43. Queen Elizabeth is also thought to have spoken Spanish, Welsh, Irish, Flemish, Greek and Cornish.

44. Elizabeth wore large gallant wigs and white makeup over her face, which was in keeping with the style of the era.

45. Like her father, Elizabeth was infamous for her propensity for colorful language.

Portrait of Elizabeth II

46. It is believed that Elizabeth swore frequently.

A castle is a large building, typically of the medieval period and a palace is a large and impressive building forming the official residence of a ruler, pope or archbishop.

47. Queen Elizabeth I owned over a dozen magnificent palaces.

Picture of Whitehall Palace

48. Elizabeth I spent a lot of time in Whitehall Palace and Richmond Palace.

29

49. Queen Elizabeth I was imprisoned in The Tower of London.

Picture of Tower of London

50. Elizabeth spent much of her childhood in The Old Palace at Hatfield.

Palaces and Castles

51. While Elizabeth spent a lot of time at Hampton Court Palace, it is widely thought to be one of her least favourite palaces.

Picture of Hampton Court Palace

52. Elizabeth caught smallpox twice at Hampton Court Palace.

31

A reign is the time during which a monarch rules.

53. The two major religions in Elizabethan England were the Catholic and Protestant.

54. Poverty was on the rise during the Elizabethan period.

55. A series of laws was introduced by the English Parliament in 1563, 1572, 1576, 1597 culminating in the 1601 Poor Law designed to make provision for the poor

Portrait of Mary I

56. Elizabeth's sister, Queen Mary was Catholic and persecuted Protestants who were burned alive for their beliefs.

33

57. Queen Elizabeth I adhered to the Protestant religion and restored Protestantism as the official religion. However, believed in religious freedom.

Portrait of Mary Queen of Scots

58. There were many Catholic plots against Queen Elizabeth I as many Catholics wanted to replace Elizabeth with her cousin Mary Queen of Scots.

59. Elizabeth's reign also saw many brave voyages of discovery, including those of Francis Drake, Walter Raleigh and Humphrey Gilbert, particularly to the Americas.

Picture of Westminster Abbey

60. Elizabeth was crowned by Owen Oglethorpe in Westminster Abbey.

Printed in Great Britain
by Amazon